Idaho

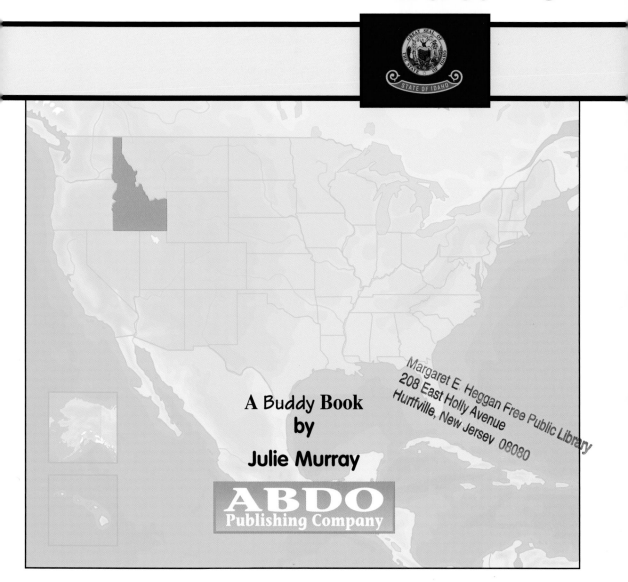

A Buddy Book
by

Julie Murray

ABDO
Publishing Company

VISIT US AT
www.abdopub.com

Published by ABDO Publishing Company, 4940 Viking Drive, Edina, Minnesota 55435.

Printed in the United States.

Edited by: Sarah Tieck
Contributing Editor: Michael P. Goecke
Graphic Design: Deb Coldiron, Maria Hosley
Image Research: Sarah Tieck
Photographs: Artville, Clipart.com, Corbis, Digital Stock, Getty Images, Library of Congress, One Mile Up, PhotoDisc, Photos.com. Special thanks to the National Scenic Byways Program (www.byways.org) for use of the photo on page 13.

Library of Congress Cataloging-in-Publication Data

Murray, Julie, 1969-
  Idaho / Julie Murray.
    p. cm. — (The United States)
  Includes bibliographical references and index.
  ISBN 1-59197-671-5
    1. Idaho—Juvenile literature. I. Title.

F746.3.M87 2005
979.6—dc22

2004056808

Table Of Contents

A Snapshot Of Idaho 4

Where Is Idaho? 7

Fun Facts 10

Cities And The Capital 12

Famous Citizens 14

The Rocky Mountains 16

Idaho Potatoes 20

Snake River 22

A History Of Idaho 28

A State Map 30

Important Words 31

Web Sites 31

Index .32

A Snapshot Of Idaho

Idaho is full of lakes, rivers, mountains, prairies, and wild animals. When people think of Idaho, they think of the state's many natural features.

There are 50 states in the United States. Every state is different. Every state has an official state nickname. Idaho is sometimes called the "Gem State." This is because natural gems such as garnets, opals, and topaz are all found there.

People visit Idaho to see scenery such as lakes, mountains, and wildflowers.

Outdoor sports like white-water rafting are popular in Idaho.

Idaho became the 43rd state on July 3, 1890. It is the 13th-largest state in the United States. It has 83,574 square miles (216,456 sq km). It is home to 1,293,953 people.

Where Is Idaho?

There are four parts of the United States. Each part is called a region. Each region is in a different area of the country. The United States Census Bureau says the four regions are the Northeast, the South, the Midwest, and the West.

Idaho is located in the West region of the United States. Idaho has four seasons. These seasons are spring, summer, fall, and winter.

Four Regions of the United States of America

ALASKA

WASHINGTON

MONTANA

NORTH DAKOTA

VERMONT

MAINE

OREGON

IDAHO

MINNESOTA

WISCONSIN

NEW HAMPSHIRE

MASSACHUSETTS

NEW YORK

RHODE ISLAND
CONNECTICUT

WYOMING

SOUTH DAKOTA

MICHIGAN

PENNSYLVANIA

NEW JERSEY

DELAWARE

NEVADA

NEBRASKA

IOWA

OHIO

Washington D.C.

MARYLAND

UTAH

COLORADO

ILLINOIS

INDIANA

WEST VIRGINIA

VIRGINIA

CALIFORNIA

KANSAS

MISSOURI

KENTUCKY

NORTH CAROLINA

ARIZONA

NEW MEXICO

OKLAHOMA

ARKANSAS

TENNESSEE

SOUTH CAROLINA

MISSISSIPPI

ALABAMA

GEORGIA

TEXAS

LOUISIANA

FLORIDA

HAWAII

West   Midwest   South   Northeast

Idaho borders six other states and the country of Canada. Nevada and Utah lie to the south. Oregon and Washington border the state to the west. Montana and Wyoming lie to the east. Canada is to the north of Idaho.

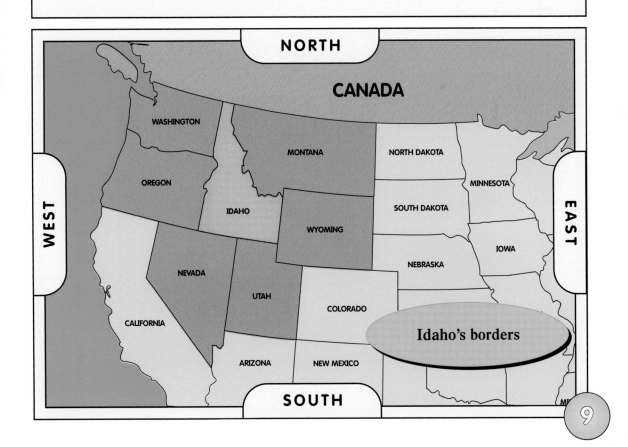

Idaho's borders

Idaho

State abbreviation: ID

State nickname: The Gem State

State capital: Boise

State motto: *Esto Perpetua* (Latin for "Let It Be Perpetual")

Statehood: July 3, 1890, 43rd state

Population: 1,293,953, ranks 39th

State flag:
Adopted in 1907

Land area: 83,574 square miles (216,456 sq km), ranks 13th

State tree: Western white pine

State song: "Here We Have Idaho"

State government: Three branches: legislative, executive, and judicial

Average July temperature: 67°F (19°C)

Average January temperature: 23°F (-5°C)

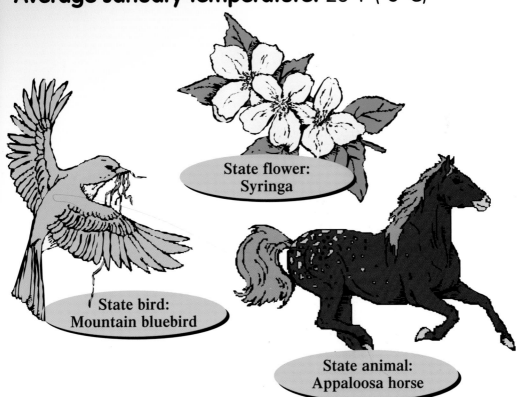

State flower:
Syringa

State bird:
Mountain bluebird

State animal:
Appaloosa horse

Cities And The Capital

Boise is Idaho's state capital and largest city. It became the state capital in 1865. Boise is on the Boise River. Boise is filled with trees. There are so many that some people call it the "City of Trees." The French word, *bois*, is where its name came from. *Bois* refers to a wooded area.

Nampa is the second-largest city in Idaho. It is near the state's southwestern border. It also is near the Snake River.

A view of Boise.

Pocatello is Idaho's third-largest city. Pocatello is located in the southeastern part of the state. Many people travel through this city on the way to the Pacific Northwest. They come by planes, trains, and cars.

Famous Citizens

Gutzon Borglum (1867–1941)

Gutzon Borglum was born in 1867 in Bear Lake. He is most famous for creating Mount Rushmore in South Dakota. His other art was well known, too. New York's Metropolitan

Gutzon Borglum helped create Mount Rushmore.

Museum bought Borglum's sculpture of the *Mares of Diomedes*. This was the first American sculpture the Metropolitan Museum ever bought.

Famous Citizens

Lana Turner (1921–1995)

Lana Turner was born in Wallace in 1921. She was an actress in films and plays. She was known for her beauty. One of her films was *The Postman Always Rings Twice*. Another

Lana Turner

was *The Three Musketeers*. Many of her films were black-and-white. *The Three Musketeers* was her first color movie.

The Rocky Mountains

The Rocky Mountains cover more than half of the land in Idaho. They are the largest mountain chain in North America. They stretch 3,000 miles (4,828 km) through the United States and Canada. They are 350 miles (563 km) wide in some places.

The highest peak in Idaho is Borah Peak. It stands at 12,662 feet (3,859 m). That is more than two miles (three km) high.

Skiing is a popular sport in Idaho's mountains.

Bighorn sheep

People traveling there can see views of the mountains. Also, people hike, bike, fish, and ride horses in the wilderness of Idaho. They also see animals such as bighorn sheep, mountain goats, elk, and bears.

Sometimes people see elk in
the wilderness of Idaho.

Idaho Potatoes

Idaho is the leading producer of potatoes in the United States. More than one-third of all potatoes grown in the United States come from this state.

Baked potatoes and French fries are made from potatoes.

Farmers grow and harvest potatoes on their farms in Idaho.

Potatoes are the most famous crop from Idaho. Idaho is known for a certain type of potato. It is called the Russet Burbank potato.

Snake River

The Snake River is the longest river in Idaho. The path of the Snake River forms part of Idaho's western border with Washington and Oregon.

There are many dams along the Snake River. These dams turn the powerful waters of the river into electricity.

This dam is on the Boise River. The Snake River has many dams like it.

Shoshone Falls is located on the Snake River. Shoshone Falls is 1,000 feet (305 m) wide. These falls drop 212 feet (65 m). Shoshone Falls is often called the "Niagara of the West." This is because it reminds people of a famous waterfall called Niagara Falls.

Shoshone Falls is one of
Idaho's main attractions.

A view of the Snake River.

The Snake River area includes Hells Canyon. Hells Canyon is the deepest gorge in the United States. It is more than one mile (two km) deep. It is deeper than the Grand Canyon.

A History Of

Idaho

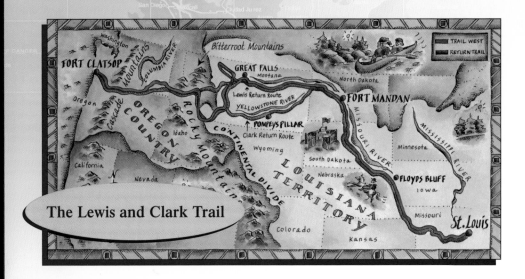

The Lewis and Clark Trail

1805: Meriwether Lewis and William Clark explore Idaho.

1860: E.D. Pierce finds gold in Orofino Creek.

1879: The first issue of the *Idaho Enterprise* newspaper is published.

1890: Idaho becomes the 43rd state on July 3.

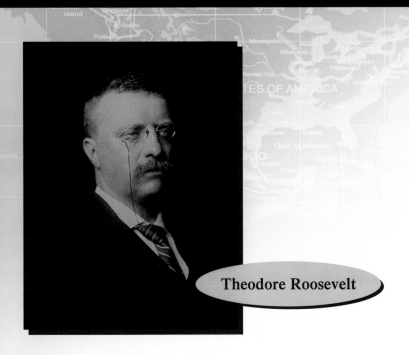

Theodore Roosevelt

1907: Theodore Roosevelt establishes the Caribou National Forest.

1927: The first Spud Day is held in Shelley.

1959: Brownlee Dam is completed.

1990: Idaho celebrates 100 years as a state.

2000: Idaho's population grows more than 28 percent according to the United States Census.

Cities in Idaho

Wallace

Lewiston

Bear Lake

Boise ★
Nampa

Sun Valley

Idaho Falls

Shelley

Pocatello

Important Words

capital a city where government leaders meet.

gorge a deep, narrow passage through high cliffs.

nickname a name that describes something special about a person or a place.

sculpture art formed from stone, wood, metal, or other materials.

Web Sites

To learn more about Idaho, visit ABDO Publishing Company on the World Wide Web. Web site links about Idaho are featured on our Book Links page. These links are routinely monitored and updated to provide the most current information available.

www.abdopub.com

Index

bear 18

Bear Lake 14

bighorn sheep 18

Boise.............................. 10, 12

Boise River........................... 12, 23

Borah Peak 16

Borglum, Gutzon 14

Brownlee Dam............................ 29

Canada................................. 9, 16

Caribou National Forest 29

Clark, William............................. 28

dams....................22, 23, 29

elk 18, 19

gems.................................. 4, 10

Hells Canyon....................... 26, 27

Idaho Enterprise 28

Lewis, Meriwether 28

Metropolitan Museum 14

Midwest 7, 8

Montana................................ 9

Mount Rushmore....................... 14

mountain goat.............................18

Nampa................................. 12

Nevada 9

Northeast 7, 8

Oregon.......................... 9, 22

Orofino Creek....................... 28

Pierce, E.D. 28

Pocatello 13

potato.......................... 20, 21

Rocky Mountains 16, 17, 18

Roosevelt, Theodore 29

Shelley 29

Shoshone Falls 24, 25

Snake River 12, 22, 23, 24, 27

South 7, 8

South Dakota 14

Turner, Lana................................ 15

United States Census Bureau 7

Utah 9

Wallace 15

Washington 9, 22

West 7, 8

Wyoming 9